Communities at Work™

Community Space

How Land and Weather Shape Communities

Angela Catalano

The Rosen Publishing Group's
PowerKids Press™
New York

For Mom and Dad for the past thirty-four years.
And for Frank, for the next thirty-four years—and beyond!

Published in 2005 by The Rosen Publishing Group, Inc.
29 East 21st Street, New York, NY 10010

Copyright © 2005 by The Rosen Publishing Group, Inc.

First Edition

Editor: Natashya Wilson
Book Design: Maria E. Melendez
Layout Design: Albert B. Hanner

Photo Credits: Cover and p. 1 © Carl & Ann Purcell/Corbis; p. 5 © Dominique Aubert/Corbis Sygma; p. 7 © Neal Hamberg/ AP World Wide; p. 9 © Geoff Crimmins/ AP World Wide; p. 11 © Morton Beebe/Corbis; p. 13 © Richard Cummins/Corbis; p. 15 © Liu Liqun/Corbis; p. 17 © George B. Diebold/Corbis; p. 19 © Peter Guttman/Corbis; p. 21 © Ed Kashi/Corbis

Library of Congress Cataloging-in-Publication Data

Catalano, Angela.
Community space : how land and weather shape communities / Angela Catalano.— 1st ed.
     v. cm. — (Communities at work)
Includes bibliographical references and index.
Contents: Community space — Living conditions — Rural communities — Urban communities — Suburbs and towns — A mountain community — An island community — A polar community — A desert community — Special communities.
ISBN 1-4042-2783-0 (lib. bdg.) — ISBN 1-4042-5022-0 (pbk.)
1. Human settlements—Juvenile literature. 2. Human beings—Effect of environment on—Juvenile literature. 3. Human beings—Effect of climate on—Juvenile literature. [1. Human settlements. 2. Human beings—Effect of environment on. 3. Human beings—Effect of climate on.] I. Title. II. Series.

HT65.C38 2005
307.1'4—dc22

                                        2003026477

Manufactured in the United States of America

Contents

Community Space

A **community** is a space where people live and work together. A community can be a school, a city, a town, or even a neighborhood.

An **environment** is everything in a space. It includes water, land, and weather. The environment may direct the type of community that can be built in a space.

The communities of Lake Inle in the Asian country of Myanmar live in a lake environment. Houses are built on poles over the lake. People have floating gardens. They use boats to get around.

Living Conditions

Different spaces have different living **conditions**. Conditions are things that can change the way people live. Sometimes people use tools to make living conditions better. A community in a snowy environment may use snowplows and tractors to keep the roads clear. A community in a dry environment may build a dam to store water.

Snowy weather changes living conditions. Roads go from dry to slippery. This makes it hard for people to get around. People use snowplows and tractors to change conditions so that roads are safer to drive on.

Rural Communities

Communities in the countryside are called **rural** communities. Rural communities have few people living on a lot of land. Often, space is used for growing food and raising animals.

Many rural farming communities form in spaces with **fertile** soil. Fertile soil is good for growing crops or grass for animals to eat.

A flat area with fertile soil is a good place for growing crops. Many farms are in spaces like this. These farmers are cutting a crop of barley. Barley is used to make bread and cereal.

Urban Communities

Cities are called **urban** communities. In a city, many people live in one area. A city must be in a space where all the people who live there can get food and water.

Many of the world's biggest cities are on coasts. These cities were built in these areas because people could bring goods in and out by boat.

San Francisco, California, is a city on a coast. Many goods are brought to and from San Francisco by boat.

Suburbs and Towns

Suburban communities, or suburbs, are communities in spaces just outside of cities. Suburbs may share a city's **resources** or they may have their own.

Towns are smaller than cities. Some towns form to support rural communities. People from the rural community come to the town to buy goods and to visit.

Suburbs often have markets where people can buy goods grown in rural communities.

PLEASE
PAY
HERE

A Mountain Community

Mountain spaces have many natural resources. They usually have plenty of water in lakes and streams. Mountains also have plenty of trees for building.

Mountain environments get many storms. The weather and the steep mountainsides can make it hard to live in a mountain space.

This is a mountain community in Yuanyang, China. From the emptiness of the other mountains you can see that this community is far away from other communities.

An Island Community

An island is land that has water all around it. Most islands must be reached by boat or airplane.

The size of an island community depends on the size of the island. Some islands have enough resources to support many communities. Some islands are only big enough for one community.

The Hawaiian Islands have communities of many different sizes. Honolulu is a city on the coast of the Hawaiian island Oahu. There are suburbs around Honolulu.

A Polar Community

Polar communities are communities in snowy, icy spaces such as the **Arctic Circle**. Polar communities are small, because polar environments are very cold and have few resources. They get little or no sunlight during the winter. Ice and snow can keep boats from bringing in supplies for much of the year. People in polar communities must wear warm clothing.

Some people in polar communities get around by snowmobile or dogsled. Today many houses in polar communities are made of wood. The wood is brought from other places.

A Desert Community

Desert spaces are dry and sandy. Days are very hot, but nights can be cold. There is little water. The sandy ground is not good for growing food.

In some desert spaces, communities move around as the people search for water. In others, the community may build a **reservoir** to store water.

These people of the Syrian Desert in the Middle East are called bedouins. They live in tents and often move from place to place to find water. The workers in the background are drilling the ground looking for water.

Special Communities

Every space has special **features** that direct what type of community can form there. People work together to build communities in all kinds of places. There is even a very small community in outer space, on the *International Space Station*. No matter where a community is, the people who live in it can help it to succeed.

Glossary

Arctic Circle (ARK-tik SUR-kul) The area around the North Pole.

community (kuh-MYOO-nih-tee) A place where people live and work together, or the people who make up such a place.

conditions (kun-DIH-shunz) The ways people or things are or the shape they are in.

environment (en-VY-ern-ment) All the living things and weather in a place.

features (FEE-churz) The special look or form of a person or a thing.

fertile (FUR-tul) Good for making and growing things.

polar (POH-lur) Having to do with the areas around the North Pole and the South Pole.

reservoir (REH-zuh-vwar) A stored body of water for a community.

resources (REE-sors-ez) Things that occur in nature and that can be used or sold, such as gold, coal, or wool.

rural (RUR-ul) Having to do with the countryside or a farming area.

suburban (suh-BER-bun) Having to do with an area of homes and businesses that is near a large city.

urban (UR-bun) Having to do with a city.

Index

Web Sites

Due to the changing nature of Internet links, PowerKids Press has developed an online list of Web sites related to the subject of this book. This site is updated regularly. Please use this link to access the list:

www.powerkidslinks.com/caw/physenvir/